ANDREW J. LAWSON

CAVE ART

SHIRE ARCHAEOLOGY

Cover photograph
Altamira, Spain. Bison are painted in red and black on the natural bosses of the
ceiling. The block beneath shows the original floor level before the cave earth was
dug away to facilitate access.
(Photograph: Juan Antonio García Castro.)

British Library Cataloguing in Publication Data:
Lawson, Andrew J. (Andrew John) *1948* —
Cave art. — (Shire archaeology, 64).
1. Stone age rock paintings. Discovery.
I. Title.
759.0113.
ISBN 0-7478-0120-7

Dedicated to Annabel, Katherine and Joanna.

Published by
SHIRE PUBLICATIONS LTD
Cromwell House, Church Street, Princes Risborough,
Buckinghamshire HP17 9AJ, UK.

Series Editor: James Dyer.

ISBN 0 7478 0120 7

First published 1991.

Printed in Great Britain by
C. I. Thomas & Sons (Haverfordwest) Ltd,
Press Buildings, Merlins Bridge, Haverfordwest, Dyfed SA61 1XF.

Contents

Acknowledgements

The author is grateful to John Wymer and Clive Gamble for their con-structive comments on the text; to Jean-Philippe Rigaud, Jean Clottes, Robert Bégouën, Jean l'Helgouach, Roger Bouillon, Jean Mazet, Louis Plassard, M Pémmandran, Mme Veyret and Luc Wahl for permission to visit caves in France; to Yannick Leguilou for his expert guidance in Pyreneen caves; to Federico Bernaldo de Quiros and Sñrs Ceballos, Domaso, Felix and Fortea Perez for making visits to caves in Spain possible; to Professor Martin Almagro Gorbea for information on Cueva del Niños; to Professor Ignacio Barandirian and Jesus Altuna for infor-mation on caves in the País Vasco; to Muriel Hammond for help with translations; and to the Trust for Wessex Archaeology for its support.

Illustrations are reproduced with the kind permission of those named in the captions.

4

List of illustrations

1
Introduction

Nothing has done more to stimulate discussion on the abilities of early man than the discovery of prehistoric cave art. The concept that he could have attained such skill was not easily grasped, because it was difficult to comprehend that while man depended upon 'crude' chipped stone for his tools, and struggled daily for his existence in the extreme climates of an ice age, he was also capable of creating a brilliant artistic tradition. Yet since the first major discovery of a painted cave, at Altamira in northern Spain in 1879, archaeologists have learnt that such art confirms the skill, subtlety and perception of the human race much earlier than the first urbanised civilisations or written documents.

This book has been written as a brief introduction to an important and intriguing subject. The topic has provoked heated debate, ingenious explanation and copious description, so it will be possible here to present only the most important facts and review only the most favoured interpretations. Although there is not a single decorated cave in Britain, contemporary archaeological deposits exist in England and Wales and a knowledge of the cave art of western Europe is essential to our full understanding of these deposits.

It is probable that the majority of readers will not have visited any decorated cave, so, to begin, two sites, closely situated but contrasting in their content, will be described.

Although it is dangerous to try to interpret cave art from descriptions and pictures alone, and most modern scholars would agree that an intimate knowledge of the caves is essential, for their form, complexity and very ambience must have influenced the creation of the art, few people have the privilege of being able to visit the decorated caves.

Niaux

The cave of Niaux is situated 5 km south-west of Tarascon-sur-Ariège in the *département* of Midi-Pyrénées in central southern France. The cave is owned by the state and is open to the public. Although the number of visitors is restricted to two hundred each day, most casual passers-by are accommodated despite promotion of the cave as a tourist attraction. The small D56 road winds from the valley floor which carries the Vicdessos, a tributary of the Ariège, to a massive cave porch at an altitude of 678 metres. The porch offers a panoramic view of the Pyrenees and can be clearly seen from the valley (figure 1). At the back of the porch the visitor passes through a small steel door and along a concrete-lined tunnel barely 2 metres high. Immediately beyond the tunnel is the vast interior of the cavern. There is no electric lighting and if it were not for the torches provided by the guide the visitor would be in absolute darkness. Similarly, all sound is absent, save the distant irregular dripping of water. The atmosphere is damp and cool, a regular temperature of 12°C usually contrasting with the warm air outside. On the left side the ground falls away across angular limestone blocks to standing water which covers most of the floor of the chamber, which is some 30 metres wide, as far as a narrow passage 50 metres distant. To the right the well trodden path leads upward into a high vaulted corridor. A few pale stalagmites contrast with the grey limestone rock. The guide leads the visitor upward into the cave: from time to time the route crosses small ridges hardened by calcite with pools of standing water between; occasionally the visitors are obliged to step nimbly from the edge of one pool to another. Half clambering, they pass another steel door. The distance of 700 metres between the entrance and the first major change of direction of the long cave seems immense despite the relatively easy walk. So far, the only adornments of the walls that the visitor has seen are the graffiti, several signed in the seventeenth century,

1. Niaux, France. Modern access to the decorated system of galleries is through the massive porch which dominates the Vicdessos valley. (Photograph: Andrew J. Lawson.)

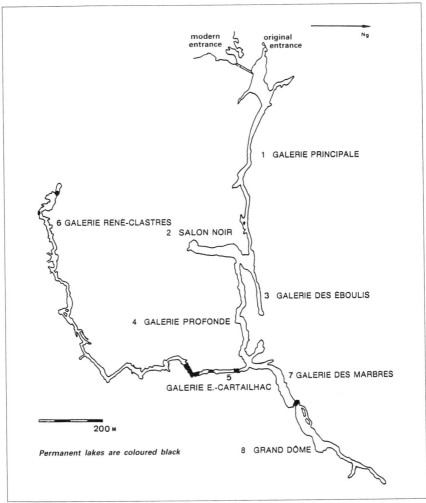

modern entrance

original entrance

Ng

1 GALERIE PRINCIPALE

6 GALERIE RENÉ-CLASTRES

2 SALON NOIR

3 GALERIE DES ÉBOULIS

4 GALERIE PROFONDE

7 GALERIE DES MARBRES

5
GALERIE E.-CARTAILHAC

200 M

Permanent lakes are coloured black

8 GRAND DÔME

2. Niaux, France. Plan of one of the largest decorated caves in the French Pyrenees. The famous black outline paintings are situated in the Salon Noir some 700 metres from the entrance. (After Jean Clottes.)

showing that easy access is not new. Nearly 500 metres from the entrance concrete posts and wire fencing apparently surround elaborate signatures, although the guide points out that the protection is really for a few small red-painted spots and lines beneath. The change of direction occurs in a vast chamber, le Grand Carrefour. Although the visitor ascends to the right into the principal painted gallery, the Salon Noir, beyond lies a network of galleries: one, the Réseau René Clastres, extends for a further kilometre (figure 2), and a second eventually connects with the outside world as the cave of Lombrives on the north-east side of the mountain.

The entrance to the Salon Noir is marked by a flat rock surface or panel (only 1.5 metres high from the floor of the right-hand wall) covered with red and black spots of paint, but beyond it three walls of the 15 by 20 metre chamber are covered with dozens of lifelike drawings of animals, in black outline (figure 3). The natural contours of the rock divide the mass of paintings into six panels. Using a contrasting technique, horse, bison and ibex have been engraved on the crust of the floor sediment at the end of the gallery. The remarkable paintings of this chamber are generally accepted as one of the most spectacular achievements of prehistoric artists. In all Niaux contains 450 representations, thus earning its title as a 'giant' amongst caves and consequently we will make frequent reference to it. Although visits to the cave had been promoted since the 1830s and a hand-made map of about 1880 (by Commander Molard) marks a 'Salle des Bêtes', the paintings were not officially discovered nor first published (by Emile Cartailhac) until 1906.

3. Niaux, France. Ibex from the Salon Noir, drawn in black. (Photograph: Jean Clottes.)

Fontanet

The cave of Fontanet is situated on the right bank of the river Ariège, 5 km south-east of Tarascon-sur-Ariège, and is the most southerly of the decorated caves in the Ariège valley. A small road, the D23, runs from the thermal spa of Ussat-les-Bains to the hamlet of Ornolac, from which a track follows the river and above which the cave opens at an altitude of 580 metres. Although the cave mouth is obvious, it is reached only after twenty minutes climbing from the valley floor. It lies beneath the land of several owners and is not open to the public: access is possible only with express permission and with the assistance of a spelaeologist. The cave has no artificial light and a miner's lamp on a hard hat is the best means of illumination, leaving hands free to clamber over the muddy surface.

The extensive cave system has been known and explored many times, but the decorated part was found by Luc Wahl only in February 1972. Behind the large cave porch the low entrance is blocked by a steel door only 1 metre high. Beyond, a narrow corridor requires the visitor to progress by squatting and crawling. Frequently the distance between the ceiling and the sandy floor is less than 1 metre, but occasionally the vault extends upwards to 5 metres. 450 metres from the entrance is a point of access to an upper gallery (named after its discoverer as the Galerie Wahl) which can be reached only by an expert climber using artificial aids and rope ladders. This opening gives access to the back of a 300 metres long gallery which, with the exception of a small median chamber, is only 3 to 5 metres wide.

This small gallery is a veritable time capsule because some 14,000 years ago it had been an open cave inhabited and decorated by palaeolithic people before it was catastrophically sealed by a landslide. The original entrance is no longer visible on the surface and is covered by a scree slope to the south of the accessible present entrance to the system. But inside nothing has been disturbed since the last visit of the palaeolithic inhabitants. Hearths, discarded bones and tools are found throughout the gravelly surface of the first 60 metres of the gallery. On a ledge 1.85 metres above the ground lies the skeleton of a salmon, as if abandoned by some expert palaeolithic fisherman. Surfaces are covered with a fine black dust, so that the cave seems even darker than others. However, this does not obscure the hearths, pale-coloured bones or the lighter walls. Deeper into the narrow passage, where fine clay covers the floor, the footprints, skid marks, handprints and doodles of the last ancient visitors are preserved. The footprints are frequently of children, one of whom was probably about six years old, while the handprints are so well preserved that even the lines of the palm can be seen. On the walls are paintings and engravings. The first on the right-

4. Fontanet, France. The first painting in the cave is a red and black painted bison, just discernible in the top left corner, situated above the discarded bones and placed cobbles which surround an intact palaeolithic hearth. (Photograph: Jean Clottes.)

hand wall, only 20 metres from the original entrance and only 1 metre above a hearth, is a bison painted in red with detail picked out in black (figure 4). This painting must have been lit originally by daylight. 20 metres further on an alcove entrance is covered with many fine engravings, mainly of bison, and black paintings including the calcite-covered image of a human-like form. Within the alcove are the paintings of strange bulbous heads, thought to be human, and of animals and spots.

Although the paintings of Fontanet are not as extensive or spectacular as Niaux (there are 230 representations in all), the incomparable preservation of archaeological remains and structures at Fontanet indicates what has unfortunately been lost at sites such as Niaux. Unwittingly the early explorers of many of the finely decorated caves have so trampled and excavated the floors and at times caused such alteration to the walls that priceless associated evidence has been lost; in so doing they have devalued the remarkable but fragile evidence of this remote period.

None of the modern visitors to Niaux will be permitted to see Fontanet. Few will realise that the gaping cave entrance of Niaux at which they arrived is not the original; the original entrance was the narrow passage at the left-hand end of the first chamber. Having seen some of the engraved animals on the floor of the Salon Noir, they may not realise what else may have been trodden on, knelt on or dug away by the seventeenth-century graffiti writers, if not before. At the Grand Carrefour only the most subtle of lighting will show where bison were once painted on flat rocks 2 metres above the floor. The paint has vanished, but in the relatively short time that it remained alteration to the rock took place so that now only a different texture to the surface where the paint was once applied indicates the designs. In 1977-8 water running over the decorated surface of the Salon Noir destroyed a large area of the paintings. The reason for this was unknown: some have blamed the damage on an ever increasing number of visitors, who by their presence alter the flow of air in the cave. Whatever the reason, the destruction shows that, despite preservation for 14,000 years and careful management, paintings can be quickly swept away. But even in Niaux discoveries continue to be made. Only in 1974 were two engraved bison and an arrow-like sign discovered in a small alcove on the right-hand wall of the Salon Noir, despite detailed survey of this area since 1906. In 1979 for some unknown reason the water levels of underground lakes within the Réseau René Clastres dropped, allowing access to the distant part. Five immaculately preserved wall paintings and nearby naked footprints were found at the end of the gallery.

But what becomes clear from an examination of these two examples is that there is a need to ensure the finest protection for newly discovered sites, while we continue to record with care the known sites and use them judiciously to educate our society on the fragility of the evidence and the achievements of palaeolithic artists. With this in mind we will examine the evidence further.

The art in question belongs to the period approximately between 35,000 BC and 10,000 BC. To many, this period (the late Pleistocene) is so remote that it is difficult to think that man then was anything more than 'a mere, squat, grunting savage'. However, we know from radiometrically dated strata in Africa that primitive forms of man had been making stone tools for more than 2 million years and that *Homo sapiens*, the modern form of man to which the cave artists belonged, evolved nearly 100,000 years ago. Between that time and the phase of cave decoration the Neanderthal form and its associated stone industries came and disappeared, so that by 35,000 BC an advanced society of hunting and gathering humans of modern form was sufficiently well established to combat the rigours of a changing climate, and especially the final extreme cold phase of the ice age (known as the late Würm stage on the continent or the Devensian stage in England). Employing the stone-blade industries of the Upper Palaeolithic, man had already sprung from the starting blocks in the accelerating race of social, philosophical and technical development towards the present day. By the end of the ice age the first artistic hurdle had not only been cleared but was being left behind as man rose to the challenge of new obstacles.

Upper Palaeolithic people decorated not only cave walls but also many of their everyday tools. Although extremely sharp cutting edges could be manufactured on flaked stone, tools for other functions were manufactured from bone, antler and doubtless wood, bark, leather and horn, but being organic these have long since decayed. These soft organic materials could easily be carved and we find the same artistic tradition expressed on them as in caves. Indeed, if one has to seek an origin for art, the earliest carved figures, dating to more than 30,000 years ago, are found in southern Germany. These Early Upper Palaeolithic carvings are small models of animals, but in the Late Upper Palaeolithic bone spear-throwers (figure 5), shaft straighteners, buttons and the like were highly decorated and have been found on many contemporary archaeological sites throughout Europe. On many sites apparently non-utilitarian flat stone tablets (plaquettes) were repeatedly decorated with animal engravings before being discarded in living places and caves (figure 6). At sites such as Enlène in the French Pyrenees the decoration of the plaquettes can be closely compared with the mural art of Les Trois Frères and Le Tuc d'Audoubert, which form parts of the same cave system through which the river Volp flows. Although in general the number of decorated objects (*art mobilier*) far outweighs that of cave art (parietal art or *art rupestre*), the purpose of this account is to review the more puzzling decoration of the caves themselves.

The practice of painting, engraving and sculpting living rock is found among hunting and gathering societies on all five continents. The reasons for doing this are as varied as the other social customs of the peoples who inhabit the various regions of our planet. But at no other time nor in any other locality has man penetrated the far recesses of pitch-black caves to express himself in such an accomplished and tangible fashion than in the late stone age of western Europe; nowhere is the tradition certainly as old. Research on other continents does not have the same long history as in Europe, but as archaeologists seek new evidence so hints emerge that very ancient art also exists elsewhere. In 1990 the complex aboriginal designs in the rock shelters of Laurie Creek in the Northern Territory of Australia were dated to about 18,000 BC. At the same time stencilled hands on the edge of daylight penetration, some 35 metres from the entrance of Judd's Cavern in southwestern Tasmania, were dated to about 8000 BC. Two other caves, Ballowine Cave and the other unnamed, in the same Karst caves of the Southern Forest region of Tasmania were found to have designs of unknown date beyond the reach of daylight. On mainland Australia a number of short lines made with a finger on the wall of Koonalda Cave are claimed to be contemporary with archaeological deposits dating back 20,000 years, while others, such as Early Man Shelter, are proven to be at least 13,000 years old. Some authors have claimed dates as early as 31,000 years ago for some of the carvings and petroglyphs in the arid parts of southern Australia, such as those of Karolta in the Olary region, but the reliability of the 'cation ratio' method used to obtain these dates is not proved. In southern Africa the Border Cave

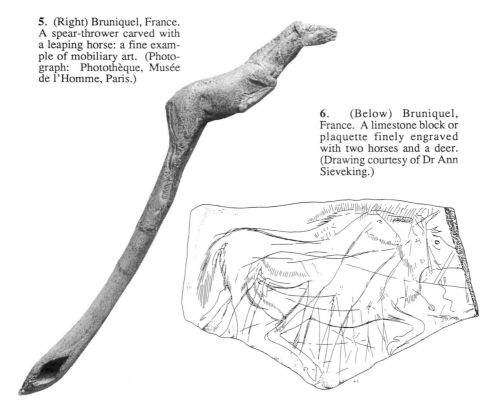

5. (Right) Bruniquel, France. A spear-thrower carved with a leaping horse: a fine example of mobiliary art. (Photograph: Photothèque, Musée de l'Homme, Paris.)

6.   (Below) Bruniquel, France. A limestone block or plaquette finely engraved with two horses and a deer. (Drawing courtesy of Dr Ann Sieveking.)

has produced bones and wood with engraved lines dated to more than 35,000 years ago, and the Apollo 11 cave in Namibia has produced a few painted stone fragments dated more than 20,000 years ago. In Algeria the site at Afala Bon Rhummel has produced a fragment of a modelled wild sheep from a deposit dated to 14,000 BC. In South America, at the cave of Pedra Furada, stone fragments with painted lines dated to at least 17,000 years ago have been discovered, although a greater antiquity has been claimed. Although each of these continents has a rich artistic tradition which in some cases continues to the present day, the origins cannot yet be proved to be as old as that of western Europe.

With the amelioration of climate after 10,000 BC, an artistic tradition which had retained some measure of unity throughout Europe for a remarkable 25,000 years ceased. In some areas, notably in central and eastern Spain, similar traditions developed in post-glacial times, while in Scandinavia new forms of rock art evolved in the lands freed from polar ice.

7. La Ferrassie, France. Naturally accumulated deposits have filled a shelter (*abri*) beneath the cliff. The section exposed by excavation contains many archaeological layers rich in stone tools, charcoal and bones. (Photograph: Andrew J. Lawson.)

But generally knowledge of the decorated caves of western Europe disappeared until a scientific interest in the creation of the earth and the evolution of the human species developed. In 1797 John Frere had watched workmen unearth flint implements from brickearth at Hoxne in Suffolk. But it was his realisation that these belonged to a 'very remote period indeed: even beyond that of the present world' which led to the first major contradiction of the previously secure biblical account of human development. When in 1823 William Buckland found stone tools with bones of mammoths and woolly rhinoceros at Paviland in West Glamorgan in Wales he could not accept that associated human bones could be 'coeval with the antediluvian bones of the extinct species'. But following the work of such pioneers as Boucher de Perthes, who published his work on the Somme gravels in 1847, the evidence for an early origin of mankind became overwhelming. By the late nineteenth century the investigation of stone age deposits in cave mouths eventually led to the startling rediscovery of long-lost artistic masterpieces.

Context

Although palaeolithic cave art is sometimes found deep in caves, it is a misconception that human communities usually lived in such a dark and potentially dangerous location. Normally they lived in the open air, constructing skin tents for shelter (such as those reconstructed at Pincevent, near Paris), or in the mouths of caves or beneath rock overhangs (such as that reconstructed at L'Abri du Blot, Cerzat, Haute-Loire) where they could seek protection from the elements but enjoy daylight. In these living places tools, food refuse, fuel ash and industrial waste accumulated (figure 7). These by-products of occupation became mixed with soil blown, washed or carried on the feet into the site. Fragments of rock from the cave roof or cliff above also fell on to the living area whilst nature contributed pollen from nearby flowers, siliceous plant remains (phytoliths), small mammal bones, snail shells and even unicellular creatures (such as ostracods) to the thickening layer. The survival of each of these classes of evidence depends upon soil acidity and seldom will all of them survive together. However, the different species represented in the floral and faunal remains and the proportions of each give a good indication of the environment prevailing at the time of deposition. Similarly, even the size of rock fragments can be used (granulometry) to gauge broadly the changes in ambient temperature. Detailed studies of these environmental indicators show that Upper Palaeolithic people successfully adapted to many different locations, climates and their consequent environments. The multi-disciplinary study of the artefacts, refuse and environmental indicators from accumulated deposits is the basis of palaeolithic archaeology.

As is the case today, different parts of Europe experienced different microclimates depending upon their latitude or geographical position, but the fluctuations of climate in the Würm/Devensian glaciation were so marked as to affect the entire continent. At the coldest period (about 19,000 years ago) the polar ice sheet stretched as far south as the Severn estuary and the Wash in England, while mountain glaciers of the Alps, Pyrenees and Cantabrian Mountains formed localised icecaps uninhabited by man. Archaeological and geological deposits of such periods yield bones of animals, some long extinct, that once roamed the tundra and grassland steppes of much of north-western Europe: these include the mammoth, woolly rhinoceros, primitive horse (Przewalski's horse), bison, reindeer, saiga antelope and many more. In warmer phases, when temperatures may have approached those of today, a woodland habitat developed in which faunas with different adaptations, including pig, wild oxen (aurochs), elk, giant deer (*Megaceros*) and red deer abounded.

Upper Palaeolithic people were totally dependent on natural resources for their food supply. They may have been able to control in a limited way the herds of horse or reindeer, but on the whole animals, fish and birds were hunted not only for their meat but for skins, antler and horn which would provide clothing and raw materials. Plants provided not only fruits, berries and edible roots, but wood, bark and wicker, all of which could be used by the hunters and gatherers for nets, rope, baskets and a whole range of wooden objects.

After 35,000 BC the appearance of burials and objects of display, the trading of raw materials and an increase in the wealth of archaeological deposits in favoured areas are taken by archaeologists to indicate an increased population, well organised into regional communities which could provide mutual support for such events as communal hunting forays. Some social gatherings may have been for ceremonies, such as the marriage of individuals from different social groups, and are likely to have been accompanied by gift exchange. At such meetings the exchange of philosophies ensured the spread of new ideas, established bonds and maintained hallowed traditions, taboos and principles. Such relationships were essential when communities might be dispersed, especially in the hostile environment of the last glaciation. The need for different groups within this society to identify with clearly recognisable symbols, sometimes in places to which groups might occasionally, seasonally or cyclically return, may have reinforced social cohesion: this may be one possible explanation for the extraordinary phenomenon of cave art.

8. Le Grand Roc, France. In earlier times the river Vézère has undercut the limestone cliffs. Today's houses stand on the sites of prehistoric shelters (*abris*). (Photograph: Andrew J. Lawson.)

Geographical distribution

Caves do not commonly occur in every form of rock but are often found in limestone, having been created over millions of years by the scouring action of subterranean rivers. In such limestone areas rivers may also have cut deeply into the soft rock, forming gorges with steep cliffs on either side. When highly charged with waters from melting glaciers, these swollen rivers sometimes undercut the cliffs, creating overhangs which would later serve as natural shelters for human settlers (figure 8). Both caves and shelters were decorated by Upper Palaeolithic artists. Indeed, it is probable that many open-air rock panels were also decorated, but few survive (Mazouco in north-east Portugal is a good example).

There is no generality in the size or form of the caves which were decorated: works of art are found, for example, in many places through the 2 km of the Niaux cave system in the French Pyrenees (above), throughout the cave only some 40 metres deep at Le Gabillou, or in the shallow shelter of Cap Blanc in Perigord. There were, however, preferences for penetrating the deep 'sanctuaries' at certain times. Some caves, such as El Pindal or Tito Bustillo in northern Spain, occur close to sea-level, while others are in mountainous terrain, like Covalanas, which overlooks the Gandara valley at 600 metres, or Sinhikole-Ko-Karbia, which opens in a cirque between the 1072 metres high Pic des Vautours and the Hasgagania plateau of the western Pyrenees between 1003 and 1059 metres.

Evidence for the tradition of mural art is largely limited to the areas in which caves and shelters occur, but the concentrations in distribution in part reflect the areas where active research has been carried out. For example, it was only the systematic searching of caves in the upper Ariège valley by Luc Wahl that led to the discovery of Fontanet, or the dedication of the Sociedad de Ciencias Aranzadi of San Sebastian that has filled a void in the distribution of caves in the País Vasco. Although a dozen sites are known in Italy and Sicily, at least one (Cuciulat) in Romania and at least one (Kapavaia) in the southern Ural Mountains of Russia, virtually all other sites in Europe are restricted to France and the Iberian peninsula (figure 9).

In France some 172 sites are recorded, with strong concentrations in the Dordogne and Lot area (64 sites) and the central Pyrenees (41 sites). One of the greatest densities of known sites occurs near Les Eyzies-de-Tayac, which nestles beneath the cliffs near the confluence of the Dordogne and Vézère rivers. Beside a minor tributary of the Vézère, the Petite Beaune, and just east of Les Eyzies, eleven decorated shelters are known in a distance of only 7 km. A small group of seven sites in the western Pyrenees is an extension of the large number of sites in the

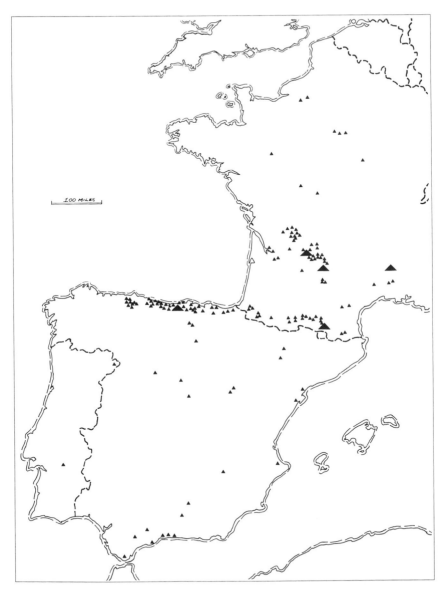

9. Distribution of decorated caves and shelters in western Europe (a small number are also known in Italy, Sicily, Romania and Russia). The larger triangles represent concentrations of sites in Perigord (including Lascaux), Lot (including Cougnac and Pech-Merle), the Ardèche gorge, the Pyrenees (including Niaux) and the Cantabrians (including Altamira). (After Baudry *et al.*, 1984, and J. A. Moure Romanillo, 1987.)

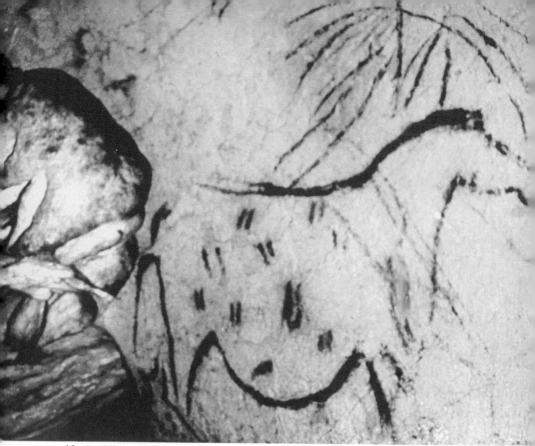

10. La Pileta, Spain. Horse drawn in black outline in one of Europe's most southerly caves. Some of the superimposed dots are in red paint. (Photograph: Juan Antonio García Castro.)

Cantabrian Mountains of northern Spain. Notable sites, such as Los Ardales, La Pileta (figure 10), Parpalló and Cueva del Niños (figure 12), are known in southern or central Spain (and one cave and one open-air site in Portugal), but of the 110 sites in the Iberian peninsula 82 occur in the extreme north: 35 in Asturias, 39 in Cantabria and eight in País Vasco and Navarra. Five of the most important decorated caves in Cantabria all form part of the same labyrinthine galleries beneath Monte Castillo outside the small former spa village of Puente Viesgo, near Santander.

No decorated sites are known in Britain. A few decorated objects are known, notably those from Creswell Crags, Derbyshire. However, decorated caves occur in northern France (Gouy, near Rouen, and Mayenne-Sciences, near Laval; see figure 11), and there is no reason why one day genuine Upper Palaeolithic cave art should not be revealed in some as yet unexplored cave or gallery in Britain, albeit that occupation of the British Isles was sparse because of the extension of the polar ice sheet.

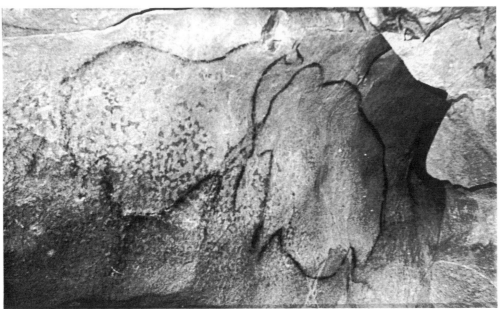

11. Mayenne-Sciences, France. A horse and mammoth drawn in black outline from one of Europe's most northerly caves. The paintings were discovered by a group of spelaeologists led by Roger Bouillon in 1967. (Photograph: John D. Herring.)

12. Cueva del Niños, Spain. Paintings from the principal decorated panel of the cave discovered in 1970 in the south-west part of the province of Albacete, central Spain. (After Martin Almagro Gorbea.)

13. Pair-non-Pair, France. From 1881 François Daleau meticulously excavated through 4 metres of sediment, revealing engravings on the walls (behind the modern door). However, these traces were not recognised as animal designs until 1896. (Photograph: Andrew J. Lawson.)

14. La Mouthe, France. Excavations in 1895 revealed a sealed passage decorated with paintings and engravings. This discovery largely led to the acceptance of the antiquity of cave art. (Photograph: Andrew J. Lawson.)

2
Discovery and acceptance

The credit for the recognition of palaeolithic cave art must go to Don Marcelino Sanz de Sautuola, a landowner who lived near Torrelavega in northern Spain, and his daughter Maria. Earlier reports of decoration in caves had been made, but it had not been recognised for what it was, nor were the discoveries publicised. Portable objects decorated with engravings had been unearthed from a number of French sites from the 1830s, most notably from Massat and Bruniquel in the 1860s, but no association with decorated cave walls had been made.

The cave of Altamira near Santillana del Mar had been discovered in 1868 and was first visited by Sautuola in 1876. During this visit he noted on the cave walls only 'a large number of repeated black lines'. By the age of 48 Don Marcelino had become fascinated by the discoveries of archaeological artefacts and decorated bones by French archaeologists (principally Edouard Piette working in the Pyrenees) and had already excavated at caves, including Revilla de Camargo. But in 1879 a second visit to Altamira, accompanied by the nine-year-old Maria, led to the discovery of the famous painted ceiling. It is said that while Sautuola excavated for artefacts just inside the cave entrance his daughter wandered off to play in the cave and looking upwards saw the now famous painted ceiling (cover picture). When the paintings were drawn to Sautuola's attention he was so enthusiastic that he could hardly speak and doubtless he was totally incredulous once the full extent of the paintings was traced with the aid of a small lamp. One of the few conversations with Maria during which the discovery was discussed was documented in 1923 and subsequently published by the German archaeologist Herbert Kühn. The discovery of Altamira has become one of the best known events in world archaeology. To quote a modern Spanish authority, García Guinea: 'There they were, patient in eternity, unmoving, filled with darkness and mystery, the now famous bison, which year after year, in massive pilgrimages, thousands of people from all over the world would come to stare at in amazement.'

The vivid ochre-red and black paintings of bison on the naturally bossed ceiling of the cave were only the most spectacular of the paintings in the cave and were far more recognisable than the simple drawings seen on the first visit. Soon afterwards Sautuola published a paper on the find, entitled *Breves apuntes sobre algunos objectos prehistoricos de la provincia de Santander*. In this he stated his conviction that the paintings were prehistoric in date. After initial interest from the authorities of the time, his claims were rejected. It was even suggested that the paintings were forged, possibly by the mute French painter Ratier, whom Sautuola had invited to his home. It is hardly surprising that a sceptical audience was not immediately convinced because the discovery was made at a time when tremendous advances were being made in science and the biblical account of creation was being challenged. Opinion was still considerably divided on the evolutionary theories put forward only twenty years earlier by Charles Darwin. Biologists, geologists and archaeologists were attempting to estimate a chronology for the events portrayed in the fossil record without the aid of radiometric dating techniques. Philosophers had to contend with the idea that the human species was a specific kind of ape rather than a divine creation, and that at an early stage of its development the species had become a creative, artistic genius.

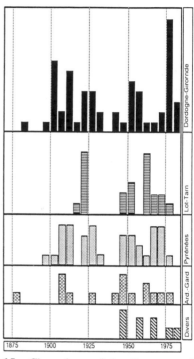

15. Chronology of the discovery of decorated caves and shelters in different regions of France. (After Dr Norbert Aujoulat.)

From 1895 onwards other painted caves were revealed in France and these altered the views of the established critics.

Engravings (at Chabot and Ebbou in the Ardèche gorge, and Pair-non-Pair near Bordeaux) and paintings (at Niaux in the Pyrenees) had been encountered in France before the discovery of La Mouthe at Les Eyzies in 1895 (figures 13 and 14). But here, as at Marsoulas in 1897, an extensively decorated cave had been choked by accumulating palaeolithic deposits: it would have been impossible for modern forgers to have entered the cave. The excavators, Gaston Berthoumeyroux and Emile Rivière, claimed them as palaeolithic, but the acknowledged authority of the time, Professor Emile Cartailhac, was satisfied only when he himself uncovered buried paintings. In 1901 details of two of the most famous decorated caves in the Dordogne, Les Combarelles and Font de Gaume, were published by Louis Capitan, Denis Peyrony and the Abbé Henri Breuil. Such finds put beyond doubt that the decoration of cave walls was as old as the flint tools and bone objects excavated from the ancient deposits in the mouths of the caves. In 1902 Emile Cartailhac published a paper entitled *Mea culpa d'un sceptique* in which he unreservedly accepted Sautuola's claims. Unfortunately the Spaniard had died fourteen years earlier.

As the authenticity of the art became accepted a deliberate search for further evidence was made. Consequently many impressive caves came to light in both France and Spain: for example, Bernifal (1903), Teyjat (1903), La Calevie (1903), La Grèze (1904) and Cap Blanc (1909) in the Dordogne; El Castillo (1903), Hornos de la Peña (1903), Covalanas (1903), La Loja (1908) and La Pasiega (1911) in northern Spain; Gargas (1904), Niaux (1906), Le Portel (1908), Le Tuc d'Audoubert (1912) and Les Trois Frères (1914) in the Pyrenees. Decorated caves continue to be found to the present day (figure 15) with the notable discoveries of Lascaux (figure 16) and Le Gabillou (1940), Cougnac (1952), Las Monedas (1952), Las Chimeneas (1953) and Rouffignac (1956). The most beautiful of the recent discoveries have been in Spain and include Altxerri (1962), Tito Bustillo (1968), Ekain (1969), Cueva del Niños (1970) and Zubialde (1990).

16. Lascaux, France. The most elaborately painted of all caves was discovered on 12th September 1940 by four local children led by Marcel Ravidat and Jacques Marsal. Here a deer, a horse, spots and a rectangular sign are painted on the calcite-covered limestone wall. (Photograph: Dr Norbert Aujoulat, Centre National de Préhistoire.)

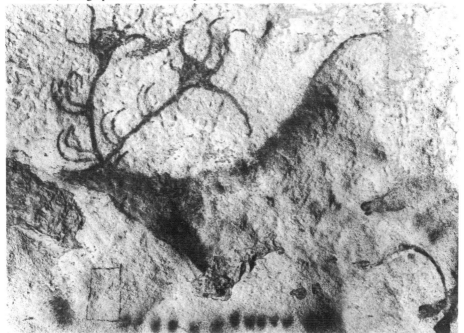

Dating

Usually the paint used in palaeolithic paintings has not itself been subject to dating techniques, although a few attempts have been made. Instead the paintings have been dated by comparison with portable objects decorated in exactly the same style. These have been found in archaeological deposits which contain flint tools of certain kinds with materials, particularly charcoal, bone or burnt clay, which can be directly dated.

Throughout the Upper Palaeolithic flint tools were created from parallel-sided, struck flint blades which were modified to obtain specialised forms for cutting, scraping or engraving, and for hafting. Many of the basic blades and techniques of production are common throughout the 25,000 years of the Upper Palaeolithic, but small numbers of distinctive forms characterise successive or geographically distinct phases (or industries, as they are called). Because these industries have been recognised on type-sites or in areas of early research, particularly in France, they have been named after the place in which they were found (for example, Aurignacian after Aurignac in France, Perigordian after the region of Perigord, or Magdalenian after the type site at La Madeleine near Les Eyzies (figure 17).

Actual dates with a small margin of error can be calculated for the charcoals or bones associated with the flint tools and occasional decorated pieces through such techniques as radiocarbon dating. Only organic materials can be used for this technique, but some methods, such as thermoluminescence, use inorganic materials. Cultural debris may have been quickly buried when a site was abandoned, only to be covered subsequently by the debris left by later occupants. On some sites these artefact-rich layers, sometimes separated by more sterile layers, have accumulated to considerable thicknesses (figure 7). Occasionally the accumulation might even completely block the entrance of the cave, as at La Mouthe (above).

We can recognise the following industries in the Upper Palaeolithic (table 1): Chatelperronian (from 35,000 BC), Aurignacian (from 32,000 BC), Gravettian (from 27,000 BC), Solutrean (from 22,000 BC) and Magdalenian (from 19,000 BC until the end of the ice age at about 10,000 BC). In some parts of France alternative names are used: the Chatelperronian and Gravettian may be referred to as the Lower and Upper Perigordian respectively. In Spain, where less research has taken place than in France, simpler divisions are put forward, so that in Cantabria the 'Early Upper Palaeolithic' equates with the French Chatelperronian, Aurignacian and Gravettian, the 'Late' with Solutrean and Magdalenian, and the 'Final' with the latest Magdalenian and early post-glacial industries.

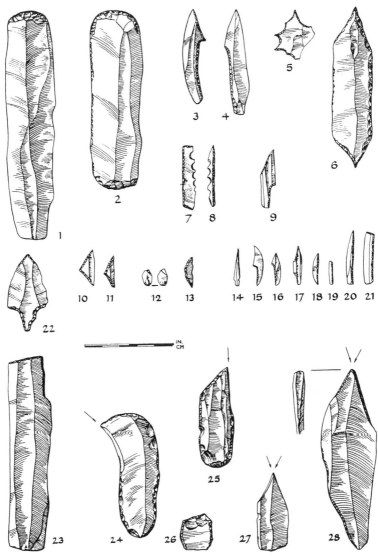

17. Characteristic Upper Palaeolithic implements from Magdalenian deposits in France: 1, end scraper; 2, double end scraper; 3, 4, shouldered points; 5, star-shaped multiple borer; 6, double borer; 7, 8, denticulated, backed microblades; 9, shouldered point on microblade; 10, 11, triangular microliths; 12, microburin; 13-21, microliths; 22, Teyjat point; 23, backed angle graver; 24, parrot-beaked graver; 25, double end scraper and obliquely backed angle graver; 26, raclette; 27, 28, dihedral gravers. (Drawing by courtesy of John Wymer; see 'Further reading', chapter 6.)

The nineteenth-century recognition of these different industries was essential in authenticating the claims for a palaeolithic date for cave art. As mentioned above, when the cave of La Mouthe was discovered in 1895 it was almost entirely blocked with an accumulation of earth containing recognisable Upper Palaeolithic artefacts, including a decorated stone lamp. Similarly, at Pair-non-Pair engravings of animals on the cave wall were discovered only after Aurignacian and Upper Perigordian layers had been dug away. At two sites at Sergeac, where overhanging rock had provided shelter to palaeolithic hunters, parts of the painted walls had become detached and incorporated into the accumulating deposit. These were subsequently covered by further deposits, which incorporated Perigordian artefacts. Clearly the painting of the walls (and detachment of the blocks) predated their burial, and a minimum age for the painting is given by the overlying Perigordian artefacts.

In more modern examples radiocarbon dating has provided a more exact date. For example, throughout the cave of Tito Bustillo in northern Spain are panels of painted animals. At the base of one such panel excavation revealed a single layer of charcoal fragments, bone and flint objects. It would seem reasonable to assume that the objects were dropped while the walls were being decorated. The radiocarbon date from the organic material from this layer, corroborated by six dates from charcoals and shells from other archaeological deposits in the cave, all of about 13,000 BC, indicates when the painting was done.

However, there are dangers in relying upon such dates. In 1970 the Réseau René Clastres (a part of the Niaux complex) was explored for the first time. Fragments of pine charcoal, presumably from primitive torches, had dropped to the sand bank near a painted panel. The charcoal gave two series of radiocarbon dates, one of dates about 10,000 years ago, the second 5000. Neither series is acceptable in dating the paintings, which are probably considerably earlier than the older series. Both series must record the intrusion of unknown visitors who gained access through a different, now blocked, entrance.

With the advent of more sophisticated technology it is now possible to date organic samples no larger than a pinhead using accelerator mass spectrometry (AMS), a technique which counts the number of atoms in a sample. In 1985 permission was granted to take minute fragments of the paint from the cave of Cougnac in France so as to date the paint directly: a black dot from the last panel in the cave, with paintings of mammoths and anthropomorphs, was sampled. In 1990 the team, led by Michel Lorblanchet, published a date of 12,350 BC for this sample, thus corroborating earlier estimates based on the associations with nearby archaeological deposits.

Table 1. Correlation of dates, flint industries, artistic styles and notable sites.

Years before present	French industries	Spanish industries	Artistic styles	French sites	Spanish sites
10,000	Azilian	Final Palaeolithic	———	Teyjat	Las Monedas
				Les Combarelles	Tito Bustillo
		———	Style IV	Bernifal	Pindal
		Late		Font de Gaume	Altamira
15,000	Magdalenian	Upper	———	Niaux	Santimamiñe
		Palaeolithic		La Mouthe	El Castillo
			Style III	Lascaux	La Pasiega
				Cougnac	Las Chimeneas
			———	Le Fourneau du Diable	Covalanas
20,000	Solutrean	———		La Grèze	La Viña
				Pair-non-Pair	Hornos de la Peña
			Style II	Laussel	Santián
				Gargas	
25,000	Gravettian	Early Upper Palaeolithic	———		
				Abri Belcayre	
				Abri Castanet	
				La Ferrassie	
30,000	Aurignacian		Style I	Abri Cellier	
			———		
35,000	Chatelperronian				

Style

When studying the decorated objects in datable deposits, and comparable illustrations on cave walls, it is obvious that style changed through time. Many people have studied and commented upon these styles, but none have dedicated their lives so single-mindedly to the subject as the Frenchmen Abbé Henri Breuil (1877-1971) and Professor André Leroi-Gourhan, who died in 1986 at the age of 74. Breuil's extensive copying of the early discoveries laid the foundation for more systematic recording and analysis by Leroi-Gourhan, whose classification is the starting point for the discussion of all recent discoveries. Although four successive styles have been defined, one blends into another and any attribution is in part a matter of opinion. Late in his life Leroi-Gourhan re-examined his division of the art and although he proposed new descriptions such as 'geometric figurative' or 'analytical figurative' he remained convinced that the earlier proposals were broadly correct, and because their titles were simpler we will use them here.

Style I is the oldest, dating from 30,000 BC, and is associated with Aurignacian industries. Because finds are rare, formal characteristics are difficult to define. Tools were not decorated at this time, but non-utilitarian stone blocks and slabs and daylit areas of cave were. Apart from realistically represented female sexual symbols, the repertoire is restricted to deeply engraved and stiffly drawn representations. Good examples are known from La Ferrassie, Abri Cellier and other shelters in the Dordogne (figures 18 and 19). Although the earliest, largely indecipherable, art in south-western France is associated with Aurignacian tools, further east naturalistically carved objects already displayed considerable artistry. For example, a figurine half lioness, half woman was found 27 metres inside the cave of Stadel in southern Germany, 1.2 metres deep in Aurignacian layers: it is dated to 30,000 BC (figure 20). Of a similar date are the carvings of a model horse and a mammoth from Vogelherd in Würtemberg.

18. (Below upper left) Abri Castanet, France. Limestone block engraved with female sexual symbols, found in Aurignacian layers and now displayed with others at the National Museum of Prehistory at Les Eyzies. (Photograph: Andrew J. Lawson.)

19. (Below lower left) Belcayre, France. Early Aurignacian (Style I) engraving of an animal on a limestone block. (Photograph: Andrew J. Lawson.)

20. (Below right) Höhle Stadel, Holenstein, Germany. Human figurine with the head of a lion carved from mammoth ivory and dating from 30,000 BC. (Photograph: Ulmer Museum, Ulm.)

21. (Left) Lespugue, France. Venus figurine with stylised and exaggerated breasts, buttocks and thighs. (Photograph: Photothèque, Musée de l'Homme, Paris.) (Right) Laussel, France. Venus figure carved on limestone, originally part of the cave wall. (Photograph: Musée d'Aquitaine, Bordeaux.)

Style II dates between at least 25,000 BC and 18,000 BC, being associated with Gravettian and early Solutrean industries. Attributed to this style are the numerous 'Venus' figurines (figure 21, left) which have been found from the Pyrenees to Kostienki or Mal'ta in Siberia, where they are dated to about 22,500 BC. These remarkable models demonstrate some measure of social unity amongst the widely dispersed hunting groups of the cold grassland steppes (figure 22). Some demonstrate a technological skill normally reserved for much later societies, namely the knowledge of baking clay to form terracotta.

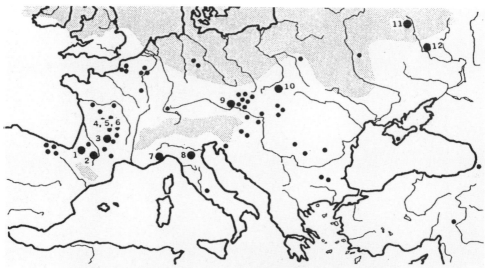

22. Distribution of so-called 'Venus figurines': 1, Brassempouy; 2, Lespugue; 3, Laugerie-Haute; 4, Sireuil; 5, Tursac; 6, Montpazier; 7, Grimaldi; 8, Savignano; 9, Willendorf; 10, Dolni-Vestonice; 11, Gagarino; 12, Kostienki. (After J. M. Gomez-Tabanera.)

23. La Grèze, France. Bison engraved in Style II low on the back wall of a small shelter, one of many decorated caves beside the Petite Beaune river near Les Eyzies. (Photograph by courtesy of Madame Veyret.)

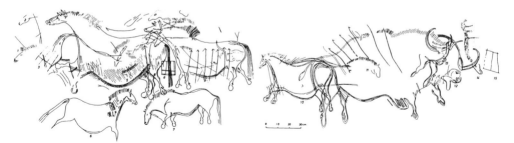

24. Lascaux, France. Paintings in Style III are found in many parts of the famous cave discovered in 1940. (Above) Horses and bison from Le Passage. (Below) Horses and cow from La Nef. (After Abbé A. Glory.)

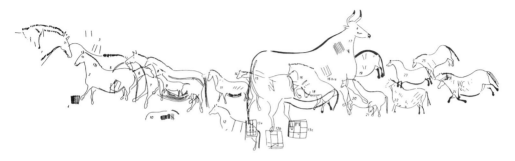

Similar female representation and other decoration are now found on tools, blocks and slabs, and in or near the daylit areas of a small number of caves (figure 21, right). Some unity in the representation of animals is seen, in particular the dependence on a strong sinuous line to define the neck and back. Horns and antlers are shown in absolute profile or with inaccurate perspective, as if seen from the front (so-called twisted perspective). Frequently the limbs are sketchy and without hooves. Good examples are found at La Grèze (figure 23) and La Mouthe in the Dordogne, Pair-non-Pair near Bordeaux, Gargas in the Pyrenees, La Viña and Hornos de la Peña in Cantabria.

Style III developed around 17,000 BC and continued until approximately 13,000 BC; it is found with later Solutrean and early Magdalenian deposits. A development from the earlier style is clear and dependence on the dorsal line is still marked. Execution displays a mastery of the stylistic convention based on the flowing dorsal line, but greater exaggeration gives power to the image. The necks of horses, bulls and ibexes are strongly arched, as are the shoulders of bison. Although hooves may be shown in detail, the limbs may be disproportionately short, so that the bodies seem oversized. Perspective is not always true:

25. Lascaux, France. The first 'Chinese horse' on the right wall of the Diverticule Axial, painted in Style III. (Early commentators thought that these paintings showed horses in a similar way to Chinese paintings.) (Photograph: Dr Norbert Aujoulat, Centre National de Préhistoire.)

frontal, profile or three-quarter views may be grafted to the structural line. The best known site where this style occurs is Lascaux (figures 24 and 25), but others include Pech-Merle (figure 26) and Cougnac in the Lot district, Covalanas and El Castillo in Cantabria.

Style IV evolved naturally from the earlier style, so that no obvious break is discernible, and dates roughly between 13,000 BC and 10,000 BC. The representations bear an almost photographic accuracy, although in some examples earlier conventions linger. Details of the animals' coats or modelling may be given, and movement in the subject breaks away from the stiff attitude of earlier sketches. The use of two or more colours in (polychrome) paintings enhances these sophisticated and expert images. More than three-quarters of the known decorated sites (and portable objects) can be attributed to this late stage. Some of the best examples include the painted ceiling at Altamira (figure 27), Las Monedas, Ekain and Tito Bustillo in northern Spain; Niaux (figure 3), Le Tuc d'Audoubert and Les Trois Frères in the Pyrenees (figure

26. Pech-Merle, France. Frieze of dappled horses in Style III, with negative handprints, a fish and other symbols. (After S. Giedion.)

27. Altamira, Spain. Plan of the painted ceiling. The complete animals are the famous 'polychrome' images, but less well known are the other symbols and fragmentary designs. The rectangular outline in the centre represents the limit of cave sediment which has not been removed from below the ceiling since the discovery. (After Miguel A. García Guinea.)

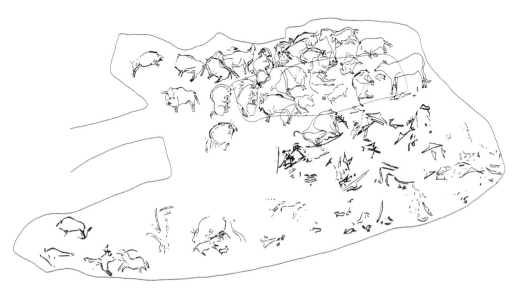

28. Les Trois Frères, France. Black outline paintings of lions in Style IV. (After Abbé H. Breuil.)

28); Teyjat, Les Combarelles and Font de Gaume in the Dordogne.

It must be stressed that stylistic conventions can offer only a guide to the date of the works of art, and authors may differ in their assessment of the same images. But some depictions are highly stylistic, whilst others are more realistic: recognition of the crucial characteristics becomes easier with familiarity with different sites in relatively close proximity. If two sites such as Gargas (Style II) and Niaux (Style IV) are visited in quick succession, the differences in style become obvious. The general content of the art (see chapter 3) is the same in different geographical regions although there are characteristics which distinguish localised traditions or styles. For example, black outline paintings are common in Style IV images in the Pyrenees. At Niaux the Style IV bison are usually drawn with a double line beneath the mane; horses have two vertical shoulder lines; there are frequently two straight lines in front of the animal as if depicting breath; arrow-like signs occur only on bison. The proportions of the drawings are very standardised: the last panel in the Salon Noir has two drawings of ibexes facing in different directions, different in size and placed at different heights. Yet by projecting transparencies of each with different enlargements, one can be made to lie exactly over the other. The paintings of Niaux are in the same style as Le Portel, 35 km away, but the horses are shown in slightly different ways. At Le Portel the detail is greater, giving an even more lifelike appearance than those at Niaux. They both reflect a common Pyrenean tradition.

29. Tito Bustillo, Spain. The principal panel of paintings. Here much of the cave wall had been repeatedly painted with red paint and animal designs superimposed in black outline, some with remarkable detail. (After R. de Balbin Behrman and J. A. Moure Romanillo.)

Some cave complexes, such as that in Monte Castillo at Puente Viesgo (including the caves of El Castillo, Las Chimeneas, Las Monedas and La Pasiega), were decorated over a long period, so that evolution of form can be suggested. These caves greatly influenced Breuil in his establishment of the evolution of style. At others several phases of decoration have led to the placing of younger work directly over older so that the former is largely obscured, and from these a relative chronology can be established. In the main panel at Tito Bustillo (figure 29) nine individual phases can be separated, but these were executed in relatively quick succession and the style remains constant.

Late Magdalenian depictions of animals are the most accurate, and it appears that the widespread tradition of animal art rapidly waned after this zenith. However, it is suggested that some schematic or degenerate renderings, such as those at Font Bargeix, Fronsac or Gouy, mark the final expressions of the tradition. The rather schematic engraved horse at Pont d'Ambon is associated with an occupation deposit dated to the tenth millennium BC, but certainly few examples of palaeolithic cave art are later.

30. Niaux, France. Horse from the Salon Noir drawn in black in Style IV. Note the short upstanding mane characteristic of Przewalski's horse. (Photograph: Jean Clottes.)

31. Cougnac, France. Figure of a man pierced with lances and superimposed on the outline of a mammoth. Compare with figure 39. (After S. Giedion.)

3
Content

The principal components of cave art are representations of animals. They are usually shown free-standing, most often motionless. Only occasionally does it appear that the animals are drawn as if galloping, rolling or, as in the case of a frieze of deer at Lascaux, swimming. Despite the rather static nature of the images, they are lifelike and accurate in details of coat, markings and sexual attributes. By contrast there is no detail of the background: individual images do not stand on any ground, nor are they set amongst trees, grass, on bare cliffs, nor alongside rivers, nor close to human habitation (see below). It appears that the representation of the beast itself was important. Such was the knowledge of the animal that through these realistic depictions the artist offers us a vivid picture of many creatures long extinct in western Europe. The archaeological deposits contain many animal bones: although a study of these can tell us the overall size, proportions or degree of sexual dimorphism of the animals, it will not tell us what the beast looked like. It was clearly the artist's intention to portray certain animals, but it is doubtful that they were aware that many of them would become extinct and that their paintings would create such a valuable record. Now experts studying the art can distinguish, for example, between horses in winter coat (as at Niaux, figure 30) and those in summer coat (all representations in northern Spain) and by comparison with the behaviour of modern herds they can suggest that some are in aggressive stance, some passive and so forth.

Humans are not commonly shown. Early in the tradition of artistic creation small human figures (especially those of women with exaggerated features; see chapter 2, figure 21) were carved in the round and later men and women occasionally occur among the repeated scratched designs on plaquettes: at La Marche (Vienne, central France) they are particularly common. However, a different emphasis in subject matter is expressed in cave art. Wizened bearded faces or ghost-like forms occasionally occur (and only about 75 occurrences of figures are known) but do not appear in large decorative friezes and standard compositions. When they do occur, the individuals may well be dead, as is apparently the case with the 'anthropomorphs' at Cougnac (figure 31) and Pech-Merle, who are bristling with arrows or spears, like St Sebastian. Early in the tradition are explicit representations of female genitalia, but less easy to date are the numerous painted hands which occasionally occur in great profusion, such as at Gargas in the Pyrenees, where at least 250 examples, including some of children, are found in a single cave. Hand

32. Gargas, France. Handprints formed by spraying paint over the hand. Here many of the fingers appear to be mutilated. (Photograph: Claude Barrière.)

signs occur in nine sites in the Pyrenees, thirteen in the Dordogne, two in the Rhône area, six in Cantabria, two in central and southern Spain and even one in Italy: their distribution is therefore very similar to that of mural art and is an integral element of it. The hands may be in negative, where paint surrounds the hand, or positive, where paint has been daubed on to the hand and then pressed on to the rock. Some apparently lack parts of fingers (figure 32), leading to speculation that the artists had suffered accidents or from leprosy, frostbite or self mutilation, or that the fingers were curled to leave a message, like some ancient masonic signal. The human hand is a simple and basic, yet powerful image capable of considerable variation, so that at Pech-Merle single curled fingers in negative are superimposed on the frieze of dappled horses, or at Santián near Santander three rows of hands with forearms are the only decoration in the cave.

Within the repertoire of animals those that probably provided meat were more commonly sketched. Definitive lists of the total numbers of depictions of each species from all caves do not exist, partly because new discoveries continue to be made, especially where new techniques are applied. At Les Trois Frères Robert Bégouën is perfecting a technique of taking latex casts from engraved areas of the floor. From the casts examined under laboratory conditions at his own Musée Bégouën at Pujol, new images and techniques of tool use are being found. The statistics used by Leroi-Gourhan for a large number of caves have been criticised because he counted only the occurrence of an animal image within a panel, not the number of times it was represented. But in 1986 Professor Denis Vialou published his re-examination of thirteen decorated caves (or parts of caves) in Ariège and this serves as a good indicator for the overall trend.

In all Vialou counts 2611 separate illustrations or 'graphic units', but 65 per cent of these are abstract or indeterminate representations. Of the remainder 33 per cent comprise animal representations and only 2 per cent human and similar signs (table 2). In this list some species (such as ibex) are more commonly represented than in other areas, such as the Dordogne, while other species (such as mammoth) are relatively under-represented in comparison with other areas.

Table 2. The occurrence of animal, human and abstract signs in the Ariège valley, according to Vialou.

1. Animals			*2. Humans*		
bison	356		man		3
horse	174		woman		1
ibex/chamois	49		human		7
bos/bovine	22		phallus		2
deer/cervid	25		vulva		3
reindeer	22		hand		5
lion	7		'monsters' and 'masks'		10
bear	7		'humanoids'		20
bird	7			*Total*	51
fish	6		*3. Signs*		
mammoth	2		dotted		274
rhinoceros	1		linear		652
unidentified	182		complex		473
	Total	860		*Total*	1399
			4. Indeterminate		301

The animals are described here in an order which reflects their overall relative frequency in cave art, starting with the most common.

Horse (figure 33) is depicted in every major assemblage. A distinctive characteristic shown in the art is a short upright mane, the dark colour of which may continue as a stripe along the back. The limit of the light colouring on the belly and legs is frequently shown, and so occasionally are horizontal stripes on the legs or vertical lines on the withers. It is usually thought that Przewalski's horse (figure 34), which is today extremely rare outside zoos, is the subspecies depicted. It is consider-

33. Les Combarelles, France. Horses and bison engraved on the cave walls. Of the three hundred engravings in this cave, discovered in 1901, about 120 are of horses. (Drawing by Abbé H. Breuil.)

ably smaller than most modern breeds. Some pictures may be of the tarpan horse, which is similarly virtually extinct in the wild but is also a native of cool dry grasslands.

European bison (*Bison bonasus*) (figure 27), which today exists only in the protected herds of eastern Poland and in zoos, is very similar to the North American buffalo. Its massive shoulders and relatively slender hindquarters are distinctive. The chin has a pronounced 'beard',

34. Przewalski's horse in summer coat, photographed in July 1990 at Marwell Zoological Park, Hampshire. Note the short upright mane and the dark, slightly banded legs. Sometimes the belly is markedly lighter in colour. (Photograph: Andrew J. Lawson.)

behind which sags the flabby skin of the throat. Some depictions suggest that palaeolithic bison had horns longer and curved differently from their modern counterparts, but this is probably artistic licence. They would have been found in a similar habitat to that of horse.

Aurochs (figure 35) is the name of the wild ox (*Bos primigenius*), a massive beast 2 metres high at the shoulders. It was a woodland dweller that did not become extinct in Britain until the bronze age, 3000 years ago, and in Europe until the seventeenth century AD. The bulls had massive forward pointing horns. The cows were more slender, with smaller horns and lighter colour, sometimes with a pale spinal stripe.

Deer are represented by both red-deer hinds (figure 36) and stags (figures 16 and 37) and form one family of animals in which sexual dimorphism is easily seen. The stags are frequently shown with fine spreading antlers with many tines. The shape of the antlers suggests that it was the red deer (*Cervus elaphus*) which frequented the forest between the glacial extremes. In colder times reindeer were more common (see below). Antler was a source of raw material for the

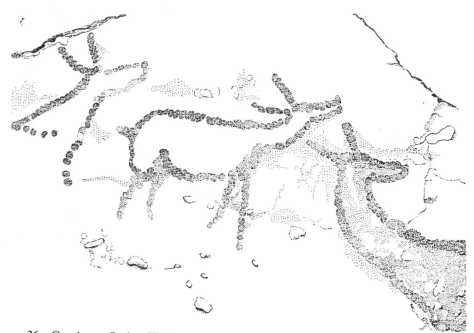

36. Covalanas, Spain. Hinds sensitively executed with a series of dots in red ochre. This site demonstrates that even sites at altitude were frequented in the Cantabrian Mountains during the later stages of the ice age. (After S. Giedion.)

manufacture of harpoons, spear-throwers and a wide range of tools. Although tough, it is easily carved, especially when softened through soaking, and in consequence the utilitarian objects could be decorated with delicate carving.

Ibex, the mountain goat (*Capra ibex*) (figure 3), is easily distinguished by its long backward curving horns. Although two different species exist, which are most easily differentiated by the curvature of their horns, it is virtually impossible to distinguish between them in parietal art. There is little evidence that any images are of the mountain sheep or mouflon, although it is closely related to ibex. The ibex naturally inhabits bare rocky mountains and must have been common in the Pyrenees and Cantabrian Mountains, where it still survives. Its depiction in other areas, such as the Dordogne and Lot, suggests that its distribution in the Upper Palaeolithic was widespread.

Reindeer (*Rangifer tarandus*) (figure 38) must have been particularly important to Upper Palaeolithic people, especially in the coldest periods. The animal, which happily devours grass in summer, is able to survive the most inhospitably cold environments by eating lichen. Frequently it

37. Las Chimeneas, Spain. Red-deer stags in black outline from one of five caves at Monte Castillo, Puente Viesgo, near Santander. (Photograph: Juan Antonio García Castro.)

38. Las Monedas, Spain. Black outline painting of a reindeer in near photographic accuracy (Style IV). The painting is orientated vertically. A horse is painted with similar vertical attitude on the adjacent rock surface of this niche in the cave wall. (Photograph: Juan Antonio García Castro.)

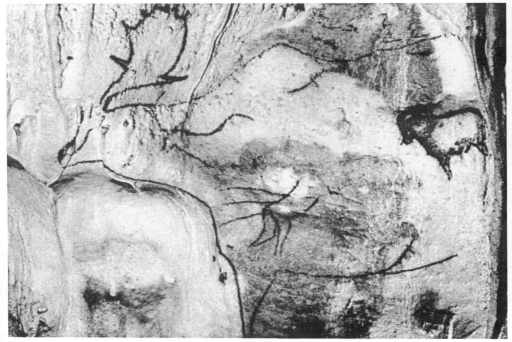

39. Cougnac, France. Giant deer (*Megaceros*) with human figure (centre), deer (above left), horse (above) and ibex (above right) within. (Photograph: Photothèque, Musée de l'Homme, Paris.)

would have represented the principal source of meat, being virtually the only game animal available, but it may also have enjoyed a semi-domesticated link with humans, as it does today with the Lapps of Finland. However, it is not commonly represented in cave art: it is known only from three caves in northern Spain (Tito Bustillo, Las Monedas and Altxerri). Here its depiction may act as a chronological indicator because it is suggested that reindeer were present only during one late phase of the last glaciation (at about 12,000 BC). Drawings of them are most easily recognised from the broad antlers, which look like the outstretched palms of hands, and from their deep muzzles.

Other game animals are represented, but rather infrequently. These include the giant deer, also known as the Irish 'elk' (*Megaceros* or *Megaloceros giganteus*) (figure 39), elk, saiga antelope, musk-ox, ass, hare and wild boar. (The only two depictions of boars are those at Altamira and some authorities consider these to be modified drawings of bison.) Many of these animals are now extinct in Europe; some have totally disappeared and are known only from their buried bones and these palaeolithic sketches.

Mammoth (figure 40) is perhaps the best known of the extinct ice age

40. Rouffignac, France. Mammoth cut into the soft clay-covered walls of the cave. The lower lines are scratches made by the claws of bears. (Photograph: Louis Plassard.)

41. Rouffignac, France. Extinct woolly rhinoceros in black outline, one of a frieze of three. (Photograph: Louis Plassard.)

42. Santimamiñe, Spain. Black outline painting of a brown bear. (Drawing after Abbé H. Breuil.)

fauna, a formidable beast standing more than 3.5 metres high. Despite their size, mammoths were frequently hunted in the open steppe conditions of the coldest phases. In the Kostienki-Borchevo region of Russia their bones were used to construct houses. The structure at Mezhirich comprises 385 bones: mandibles and long bones had been placed upright against a tent covering and tusks held the roof framework. Their physical appearance is known from a number of extraordinary finds in Siberia where animals that became trapped in permafrost more than 10,000 years ago have been released from their temporary frozen graves. These finds and the details from cave art confirm the characteristics of this giant pachyderm, with high-domed head, arched shoulders, sloping back, gently curved tusks and long shaggy coat. Some authors have claimed that other species of straight-tusked elephant are represented, particularly in the Spanish art, but these claims cannot be substantiated.

Rhinoceros (figure 41) is the second pachyderm to be represented, albeit rarely. The woolly rhinoceros (*Coelodonta antiquitatis*) was adapted to Arctic life in the same way as the mammoth. It is identified from its long nose horn set far forward of the second, shorter horn, and from the low-slung head necessary for its grazing feeding habits. Like the mammoth, it too had a coat of long hair, and examples have been found in the frozen wastes of Siberia.

In comparison with the number of hunted animals the predators are rare. Most common are bear (figure 42) and lion (figure 28), although a fox has been engraved at Altxerri and a wolf at Les Combarelles. The lions are probably cave lions (*Panthera spelea*) and the bears brown bears (*Ursus arctos*), not the gigantic cave bears which had become extinct by about 40,000 BC. In addition to these mammals the repertoire very occasionally includes fishes (for example at Pech-Merle, La Pileta, Altxerri or El Pindal) and birds (for example at Les Trois Frères).

Symbols

Less easy to interpret are a large number of abstract symbols which frequently occur within decorated caves. These symbols may be set alongside (as at Lascaux) or superimposed on animal representations (as at Font de Gaume); they may stand alone (as at La Mouthe) or in panels dedicated to their depiction (as at El Castillo; figure 43). Although great variety in these symbols exists, and no two are exactly alike, repetitive forms can be identified which appear to have some chronological and geographical significance (figure 44).

Gridiron-like signs are relatively early (found in Perigord; but they do not occur in Spain). Club-shaped (claviform) signs may have derived in later stages as simplified representations of women, which occur from almost the earliest stages of the art. In the latest stages the symbols may be trapezoidal or shield-shaped (scutiform). Tent-shaped forms (tectiforms) are found near Les Eyzies, and bird-like forms (aviforms) in Quercy.

Much more simple are panels or rows of dots, or larger spots. These frequently mark the beginning or end of panels of decoration: for example, just before the famous chamber with black paintings, the Salon Noir, at Niaux a small rock projection is covered with dots in varying shades of red and in black, as if warning or guiding the visitor to the nearby artwork. Other signs are simple lines or V-shaped arrows.

These signs have been interpreted as huts, spirit houses, tents, sexual symbols or subconscious images seen in trance (phosphene or entoptic images). However, in comparison with the naturalistic animal images they appear to represent a totally different and unexplained symbolism or iconography.

43. El Castillo, Spain. Quadrilateral signs and rows of dots, part of a panel devoted to symbols in one of the five caves at Puente Viesgo, near Santander. (Photograph: Juan Antonio García Castro.)

44. Symbols from different regions: 1-4, quadrilaterals, and 5-12, tectiforms, from Perigord; 13-14, claviforms from Lot; 15-18, claviforms from Perigord; 19-28, quadrilaterals from Cantabria. (After A. Leroi-Gourhan.)

Tools and techniques

Cave artists painted, engraved and sculpted. These techniques and combinations of them vary through time and by geographical region. For example, in the earliest phases sculpture and engraving predominate and painting is rare. At the later famous cave of Lascaux engraving is even more widespread than the colourful polychrome paintings.

Vialou's work in the Ariège shows the relative proportions of the different techniques used in that area: of the 860 animal representations, 615 are engraved, 177 are painted, 32 are imprints, four are modelled figures and 32 are painted and engraved. At different times in the Upper Palaeolithic every grade between fine engraving and deep relief sculpture was practised. In many caves today only engraving or sculpture survives, although it is possible that contemporary paintings eroded with the passage of time. Engravings may employ delicate lines incised with flint points or chisel-like tools (burins), as at Teyjat or Les Combarelles. It may employ deep carving, as at Pair-non-Pair, which may have been executed with picks. The more rock that was removed the greater the relief that could be developed in the subject. Low relief carving is well illustrated at Laussel or Le Fourneau du Diable (figure 45). These examples and other examples of high relief, such as the frieze at Cap Blanc, are restricted to Perigord.

In some caves a soft clayey surface to the cave walls has been tooled, as at Rouffignac, where images of mammoth predominate. Here and elsewhere meandering lines like boiled macaroni have been made with fingers in the soft clay. At a very few sites in the Pyrenees clay from the cave floor has been shaped into animal forms, as at Bédeilhac. Arguably the most impressive of all examples of palaeolithic fine art are the unique

45. Le Fourneau du Diable, France. Low relief sculpture of wild oxen on the edge of a limestone block which was originally set within a tented structure beneath the cave wall. (Photograph: Andrew J. Lawson.)

46. Le Tuc d'Audoubert, France. The only example of free-standing modelled clay bison, found deep within the Volp cave system in the central French Pyrenees. (Photograph: Robert Bégouën.)

group of three modelled bison at the end of the cave of Le Tuc d'Audoubert (figure 46). A fourth, engraved, figure lay next to the models on the floor of the cave, which forms part of an interconnecting series of galleries that includes the caves of Les Trois Frères and Enlène and hence is perhaps the most elaborately decorated cave system yet known.

Painters used the colours of naturally occurring pigments within the cave. Iron oxides found as ochre could be used for red, brown and yellow paint, and manganese dioxide or charcoal for black. (It is the charcoal content of some paints that has enabled radiocarbon dates to be derived from small samples [above], and the isolation of blood used in aboriginal paintings that has likewise led to the direct dating of paintings in northern Australia and Tasmania.) These pigments were commonly ground to a powder and mixed with water to create a smooth paste. It has been suggested that other additives, such as fat or egg-white, were used to bind the paint, but until 1989 no analysis had been able to prove the point, and experiments had cast doubt on the use of any medium other than water. However, in that year 59 specimens of paint were taken from black and red animal paintings and signs at Niaux. The main discovery was that the paint had been created by mixing the pigments with some form of mineral extender and binder. This had already been noted in the late 1970s at Lascaux. The finely ground mineral extender enabled the paint to adhere better to the wall and prevented cracking. At Niaux four different paint recipes were used in different periods and used the following extenders: talc; a mixture of barytes and potassium feldspar; potassium feldspar alone; potassium feldspar mixed with an excess of biotite. In the Salon Noir (but only there) the artists first sketched the animals with charcoal before applying a layer of paint. It had already been noticed that in at least one instance black paint covered a previously red-brown coloured bison, but it is hoped that the new analyses will enable a more accurate assessment of the phasing of painting throughout the cave to be made.

The paint was applied with the fingers, a brush or a wad. Occasionally the diffuse nature of the paint application leads to the suggestion that it had been sprayed from the mouth or a tube, or that powdered pigment had been blown from the fingers on to a moist surface. In the case of manganese dioxide care would have to be taken because even if less than 10 mg was swallowed serious sickness would result.

Frequently a single colour was used to draw the outline of the animal and any details of markings: sometimes lines of individual dots cleverly depicted the animal, as at Covalanas (figure 36) or Marsoulas. Sometimes the outline was infilled with a uniform wash. During the later phases two or more colours were combined with the natural hue of the cave wall or ceiling to create a polychrome effect. This technique is uncommon, only seven representations occurring, for example, in the full 2611 'graphic units' of the Ariège. But it is seen to full effect in the most famous and beautiful designs at Lascaux and Altamira, and also in a limited number of others, such as Font de Gaume, El Castillo or Ekain. In the most extensive panel at Tito Bustillo the entire surface of the wall received a red wash on to which horses and reindeer were sketched in black: this was repeated at least once, covering existing paintings (figure 29). At many sites a combination of painting and engraving is evident, or painting was used to translate the natural shape of stalagmites or boulders into those of animals. At El Castillo the natural contours of one stalagmite have been picked out with black paint to suggest a bison, while the top of the stalagmite has been shaped so that viewed from the opposite side it gives the profile of an ibex. The evidence from sites such as Lascaux for the combination of techniques has reinforced the suggestion that in those caves where only engravings are preserved paint once existed but has perished. Within any cave different techniques or combinations of techniques may have been employed. At Bernifal, where a wide variety of animal species and standardised tectiform signs are used, both engraving and the use of natural shapes are seen, as well as the use of red and black paint. By contrast, at le Gabillou almost the only technique was engraving, while in the Pyrenees many sites, such as Niaux, concentrate on the use of black paint.

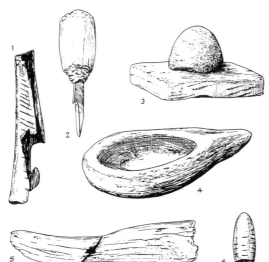

47. Tools of the artist's trade: 1, bone paint tube; 2, reconstructed engraving tool, set with resin into wooden handle; 3, stone plaque and pebble pestle for grinding pigment; 4, limestone lamp; 5, mammoth rib used as palette; 6, red ochre crayon. (Drawing courtesy of John Wymer; see 'Further reading', chapter 6.)

The abilities of cave artists seem all the more remarkable when works of art appear in the darkest recesses of deep caves. No evidence of sooting exists to support the suggestion that large fires were lit to illuminate the chamber while the artists worked. On the contrary, only small bowl-shaped lamps, which doubtless once held fat and wicks, have been found in archaeological layers (for example, 105 lamps in all have been found in Perigord), at times associated with other tools of the trade and pigment (figure 47). Very occasionally, as is the case at Labastide, a hearth is found. The evidence suggests that the works of art were executed by small groups of people who occasionally visited to decorate with skill and expedition. In the 'black frieze' at Pech-Merle three episodes of painting can be distinguished: one horse and four bison were centrally placed, then eleven mammoths surrounding them, and finally four oxen to one side. But close examination of each line and the form of the detailed feet suggests that the paintings were done rapidly by a single artist. Michel Lorblanchet, who has experimentally replicated paintings from Pech-Merle, estimates that, whereas the 'black frieze' may have taken only one to one and a half hours to complete, the panel of dappled horses may have taken five or six days. Although the latest evidence from Niaux shows that the paintings were not created all at once, the episodes of sketching in charcoal and later embellishment with different paints may have been separated by considerable periods of time and the different paints created by different artists. Rarely, as at Lascaux, where postholes and rope impressions have been recorded, scaffolding was used to enable the artists to reach levels beyond the reach of even the tallest person. Such labours must have demanded considerable investment in time.

4
Interpretation

Works of art are found in many different locations within caves: sometimes near the mouth in natural daylight, in the main gallery of a cave, inside passages, or in niches reached only with the greatest discomfort and effort, even requiring passage through subterranean lakes or siphons. Most commonly the walls form the 'canvas', but occasionally the floor is used (as at Bédeilhac), while some of the most impressive works occur on the ceiling, as at Altamira, Lascaux or Rouffignac. It is not uncommon to find that one has to lie on one's back and slither into low recesses to examine drawings, as at Hornos de la Peña, for example. Indeed, before the floor level was lowered in modern times, parts of the ceiling at Altamira were little more than a metre high.

It is possible that many daylit areas were once decorated but erosion has taken its toll. Many of the relief carvings, such as in the shelter of Cap Blanc, have, however, survived to prove the case. At the Abri Labatut (and other shelters) at Sergeac detached parts of a painted and engraved frieze were discovered in the accumulated deposits of the shelter, indicating that the ceiling was once decorated. Similarly, in the summer of 1990 fragments of the engraved cave ceiling at Le Placard were found between two layers of the Solutrean deposit beneath. At the cave of Fontanet in the Pyrenees paintings begin less than 20 metres from the original entrance, which later became blocked by boulders.

Generally, decoration deep within a cave is likely to be of a later date and in more accurate styles (III and IV; see chapter 2). 20,000 years ago most decoration was executed on shelter walls, at cave entrances or in the half-lit area beyond. In comparison, the great majority of the highly decorated chambers in unlit areas date from the centuries around 15,000 years ago. This date correlates with the final prolonged cold phase of the ice age (Würm IV), after which decoration is found once more in the more accessible areas near the cave mouth, as at Tito Bustillo.

Composition

Few decorated caves appear to illustrate scenes from life. Occasionally animals may be drawn confronting each other, as in the paired reindeer at Font de Gaume, or the lines of polychrome bison in the same gallery and of black mammoths at Rouffignac. At Font de Gaume colours are also deliberately chosen so that red and black bison and reindeer are paired.

However, at first glance many of the most lavishly decorated friezes appear as a jumble of designs. Animals of different species appear at different scales and in different colours, orientated in different directions, even vertically or upside down, some complete, others without heads or extremities; many are superimposed. From the stylistic conventions used we can deduce that some caves, such as El Castillo, were visited and decorated over many millennia. But at other caves, such as Tito Bustillo, though different phases of decoration are evident, the same style is used throughout and only a short time interval covers all the work.

The late Professor André Leroi-Gourhan demonstrated, however, that order could be discerned in the apparent random mélange of figures in complex caves. In analysing the cave of Le Portel he followed the suggestion put forward by Annette Laming-Emperaire for Lascaux that certain species represented in the cave art were always found together, or complementing each other. In particular horses, which make up to 30 per cent of all representations, complemented bison or aurochs, which also make up nearly 30 per cent of all representations. Very few caves do not have these species represented (Cougnac is one). He also divided caves into zones: entrance, central, side chambers and dark ends. His analysis showed that nine-tenths of horses, bison and aurochs were found in the central zone; most deer, ibex and mammoths (30 per cent of all representations) occurred on the periphery of the central zone or near the entrance; animal representations of bears, lions and rhinoceros (10 per cent of all representations) occurred in remote places, especially the dark ends. Leroi-Gourhan maintained that this formula was understood by the artists and was upheld throughout the life of the cave. In his terms the whole cave represented a 'mythogram', each panel an 'ideogram' and each image a 'pictogram': to him the ceiling at Rouffignac was a multi-dimensional mythogram. Although Leroi-Gourhan postulated a preconceived plan for each cave, this is often not immediately apparent because cave morphology is frequently complex, if not tortuous. The original entrances may not be known and the inventory may be incomplete. Although it would be an oversimplification to prescribe a set formula for all caves, because great variety of composition exists, it is clear that only a restricted number of animals were depicted in certain caves, and that their position for representation was carefully selected.

Selectivity

It may be obvious from what has already been said that the repertoire of cave art is limited and selective: not all the animals of the local fauna were represented and those that do appear may have different habitats. At sites where excavation has revealed archaeological layers containing bones contemporary with the artwork comparisons can be made between the species represented in the deposits and in the art (table 3).

Table 3. Comparison of percentages of contemporary animal bones and art depictions from two Spanish caves. (After Altuna, 1983.)

(percentages)	*Tito Bustillo (Levels I and II)*		*Ekain (Levels VI and VII)*	
	bones	art	bones	art
horse	3.6	37.5	0.6	57.6
bison/ox	1.1	8.4	1.2	18.6
ibex	10.7	12.5	23.7	8.5
red deer	82.7	31.9	68.7	5.1
reindeer	0.1	9.7	0.4	0
other	1.8	0	5.4	10.2

In these comparisons horse and bison/oxen are more commonly represented in the art than in the food refuse, while red deer is relatively under-represented in the art. Reindeer appears to have been rare at all times in Spain. By comparison, at certain times it was plentiful in France (98 per cent of the identifiable bone in the Perigordian IV layers at L'Abri Pataud), although it was not commonly represented in cave art. Some animals are either absent altogether in the art or very seldom represented, such as wolf, hyena and boar, while other species appear in mobiliary art but not in cave art, such as chamois, snakes, frogs and even grasshoppers. Different signs are seen in mobiliary art, but the same selectivity is also apparent: for example, at Gönnersdorf in Germany reindeer is abundant among the bones but absent from the art, and conversely lion and seal are among the drawings but absent from the bones.

Meaning

Many ideas have been put forward to explain why prehistoric people went to such lengths to express themselves in this elaborate and spectacular fashion. Because much art is located deep within caves, sometimes in difficult and dangerous settings, it was obviously not done purely for amusement or to satisfy a need for artistic expression: it is not the equivalent of palaeolithic wallpaper. The careful selection and opposition of certain animals show that the compositions are not apparently a true picture of the landscape and its creatures. Because the art has no obvious meaning, many have sought magical, ideological, religious or metaphysical interpretations, including Professor Leroi-Gourhan's 'mythogram'. Some of these ideas are drawn from the practices of modern peoples who still paint the living rock, or did until recently.

The animal designs might be allegoric or metaphoric: that is, they may appear to be one thing but are understood to be another. In this way the *Agnus Dei* (the Lamb of God) is reverently shown in Christian churches not to depict a sheep but because it has a much deeper meaning; or a dove may be painted to represent the Holy Spirit in the symbolism of the Christian Church.

It is not the intention of this introductory book to analyse, support or reject these different and often complicated theories (but see 'Further reading', chapter 6). However, the briefest description of the more persuasive ideas will give the reader an indication of the diversity of thought on the subject.

By drawing an animal control is exerted over it. This is the basis of sympathetic magic and may be invoked for different reasons: to ensure success in hunting (here symbols or signs would be seen as arrows or traps); to guarantee fertility (advocates of this interpretation would see the oversized bodies of depicted animals as evidence of pregnancy); to safeguard the food supply necessary for survival.

Totemism has been seen as a fundamental religious expression, although the forms of beliefs from different peoples described under this heading are very diverse. A totem was the representation of an animal or figure that was used as the emblem of a group of people. The animal was thought to have a special ancestral or fraternal link with the group and was synonymous with it in both the natural and the spirit worlds. Other social, religious and matrimonial customs involved the use of totems. In cave art different animals might have been drawn by different groups with allegiance to those animals which had been chosen as their totems.

Study of the cave of Lascaux led Annette Laming-Emperaire to suggest that there was basic dualism in the art. This idea was developed by André Leroi-Gourhan, first at Le Portel, but later he saw a more universal application. One group of animals was dominated by representations of horse, the second by bison or aurochs. One always complemented the other and these were thought to represent two basic principles. At Pech-Merle it could be demonstrated from the representations on a single panel that images of women were little different from those of stylised bison. From such evidence it was hypothesised that the two principles represented male and female, the former expressed as horses, the latter as bison. In this equation even symbols were associated with one or other group: V-signs were not wounds or spears, but male symbols. Even the cave itself might be female in the absence of animals to complement the drawn male-attributed animals. Around this central dualism the entire art within a cave was structured and perpetuated. The sexual connotations of this interpretation are not accepted by many archaeologists and, while statistics may prove that horse and bovids predominate, other principles that these might represent can be put forward, such as good and bad, left and right, *et cetera.*

In trance or hallucination a shaman might pass to the spirit world and adopt the mantle and powers of a revered animal. By drawing the memory of the trance, its tale could be graphically illustrated and belief in its message instilled. Paintings of beings, half animal, half human, as at Les Trois Frères or Fontanet, may represent shamans passing from the real to the spirit world. Even some of the symbols of palaeolithic art might be a record of the geometric patterns seen as the human mind passes into subconscious (so-called entoptic forms). In southern Africa Bushmen in trance induced by rhythmical dancing aspire to become the largest of the antelope, the eland, and the frequent representation of this animal in rock-shelter art is thought to portray dream sequences. Professor David Lewis-Williams has successfully linked accounts of Bushmen beliefs recorded by early European settlers with the scenes painted in rock shelters of the Drakensberg mountains of Natal, making the interpretation compelling. Unlike the Natal paintings, much of known Upper Palaeolithic art occurs in dark caves. Entoptic forms can also be experienced when a person is confined in darkness. Hence, although the South African and European art may be millennia apart, and the philosophy behind them different, they may both be a record of similar trance experiences.

The inaccessibility of some art and the lack of scattered contemporary debris suggests that deep caves were penetrated on rare occasions. Bearing in mind the dangers of venturing into a dark cave possibly inhabited by large carnivores, with only the uncertain light of a flickering lamp, the art may have been created and used only on special occasions. From the presence of children's footprints and bearing in mind the inherent dangers of exploring caves, we might hypothesise that the art was created during initiation ceremonies when young people had to pass a test of bravery before being classed as adult. What role the art played in such ceremonies can only be guessed at, but each animal might have been drawn by the representative of a certain social group who knew where in relation to the other depicted animals he or she should leave a 'signature' in the form of an animal emblem of their group. The pattern of such ceremonies would be learned by the initiated so that similar ceremonies could be performed at different locations. Because the need to respect the locations of the animal symbols and what these represented within the cave would also be learned, the record of earlier visits in the form of previous paintings would be taken into account, but the general pattern repeated. Whatever these ceremonies may have been, they have left no trace other than in the art, occasional footprints and a few hearths, leaving us to speculate on their meaning.

The large herds of game that once roamed the European countryside and woodland have now disappeared, denying us the opportunity of studying the behaviour of the animals so accurately depicted. It is now impossible to examine the interrelationship of herds of different animals that once shared the same habitat, or the social behaviour within individual herds. African game animals respect each other in predictable ways, but we cannot safely extrapolate from modern African species the behaviour of those of a different continent and a lost era. It is possible that the structure of the cave art is a narrative on such animal behaviour, created by those who daily observed it. Human survival depended on an ability to hunt, but also to conserve the food resource. The teaching of skills would be essential, while prowess in hunting would doubtless have been the basis for heroism and admiration.

When studying cave art it is easy to become distracted by the unusual and to overlook the general trend. The deep 'sanctuary' of Niaux is memorable because of the distance of the Salon Noir from the entrance. But these deep areas were favoured only at one particular time and much of the art is far more accessible. Sites like Fontanet and the decorated portable objects remind us that art was a part of everyday life. If the symbols were religious, the religion pervaded all aspects of life, albeit that certain places may have been set aside for special purposes. At Fontanet, a red and black painted bison overlooks a hearth in a daylit area but the side chamber covered with animal figures, half-animal half-human figures and human-like heads has no practical function in the dark part of the cave. Because of the variety of compositions, situations and styles in the art it would be dangerous to attach a single interpretation to it all. Several complex meanings may be interwoven but, without obvious explanation, these are impossible to unravel.

For those who study the archaeological deposits and artefacts left by the hunter-gatherers of the last ice age nothing brings them closer to the mind and spirit of palaeolithic man than his carefully and lovingly executed cave art. We can admire its beauty and skill, although we may never know its meaning: as with some ancient manuscript, we can see the words but we do not understand the language.

48. La Pasiega, Santander, Spain. A group of signs usually described as the 'inscription'. Total length 56 cm. (From Sieveking, 1979.)

5
Places to visit

The majority of decorated caves are not open to the public. They are classified as sites of national importance and are closed with protective doors. These measures have been taken in the light of experience. The introduction of visitors to most caves alters the stable conditions within the caves, which have preserved the decoration for thousands of years. Bacteria or fungi which attack paintings may be introduced; the humidity level may be altered, or inadvertent abrasion of decorated surfaces may occur. The very movement of air can cause damage to the fragile surface. More despicably, caves have frequently been vandalised despite the most stringent security. Hence we must accept with regret that, in order to preserve these fragile works of art for future generations, the public must be denied access to all but a few sites. Nonetheless, those open to the public form a representative selection displaying a good range of decorative techniques and a variety of contexts.

The following list comprises sites open to the public. Because the price of admission, the numbers of visitors permitted and the hours of opening vary, they are not quoted here. In addition to the charge for admission, tipping is expected. The caves may be open for only two hours each morning and afternoon, and in winter they are frequently shut altogether. Details of opening hours in France are given in the relevant Michelin *Green Guide* or may be obtained from the local *syndicat d'initiative*. Visitors are always accompanied by guides, who do not usually speak English. Photography is strictly forbidden, but transparencies, postcards and guidebooks are frequently available at the site or in nearby towns. Most of these sites are marked on the 1:200,000 Michelin maps of France or the Firestone maps of Spain.

In the following list the sites marked with an asterisk (*) are arguably the best examples.

FRANCE
Ariège
Bédeilhac, Foix: painting, engraving, modelling.
Niaux, Foix: painting, engraving on floor*.

Dordogne
Bara-Bahau, Le Bugue: engraving.
Bernifal, Meyrals: engraving and painting.
Cap Blanc, Marquay: relief sculpture*.
Les Combarelles, Les Eyzies: engravings*.

Font de Gaume, Les Eyzies: polychrome painting*.
Grotte de la Mairie, Teyjat: engraving.
Lascaux II, Montignac: facsimile of paintings*.
La Mouthe, Les Eyzies: painting and engraving.
Rouffignac: engraving and painting.
Saint Cirq, Le Bugue: engraving.
Villars: painting.

Gironde
Pair-non-Pair, Prignac-et-Marcamps: engraving.

Hautes-Pyrénées
Gargas, Aventignac: painting and engraving.

Lot
Cougnac, Gourdon: painting.
Les Merveilles, Rocamadour: painting.
Pech-Merle, Cabrarets, painting*.

Pyrénées Atlantiques
Isturitz: painting and low relief.

SPAIN
Asturias
El Buxu, Cardes: engraving.
La Peña de Candamo, San Roman: painting and engraving.
El Pindal, Pimiango: painting.
Tito Bustillo, Ribadasella: painting and engraving*.

Cantabria
El Castillo, Puente Viesgo: painting*.
Covalanas, Ramales de la Victoria: painting.
Hornos de la Peña, Tarriba: painting and engraving.
Las Monedas, Puente Viesgo: painting.
Santián, Puente Arce: painting.

País Vasco
Santimamiñe, Guernica: painting.

6
Further reading

Bahn, P., and Vertut, J. *Images of the Ice Age*. Windward, 1988. An excellent general survey of palaeolithic art with magnificent photographs.

Baudry, M. T. (editor). *L'Art des Cavernes*. Imprimerie Nationale, 1989. An atlas with details of every decorated cave in France.

Breuil, H. *Four Hundred Centuries of Cave Art*. Montignac, 1952. A classic review and interpretation of cave art.

Gamble, C. *The Palaeolithic Settlement of Europe*. Cambridge University Press, 1986. A review of the evidence.

García Castro, J. A. (editor). *Arte Rupestre en Espana*. Revista de Arqueologia, 1987. A Spanish survey of the decorated caves and shelters in the different regions of Spain, with excellent photographs.

Leroi Gourhan, A. *The Art of Prehistoric Man in Western Europe*. Thames and Hudson, 1968. A major work that describes the most important works and analyses the subject.

Pfeiffer, J. *The Creative Explosion*. Harper and Row, 1982. Includes interpretations based on rites of initiation.

Sieveking, A. *The Cave Artists*. Thames and Hudson, 1979. A review from one of England's foremost scholars.

Stuart, A. *Life in the Ice Age*. Shire, 1988. An introduction to the changing environments of the ice age.

Sutcliffe, A. J. *On the Track of Ice Age Mammals*. British Museum (Natural History), 1986. A description of the evidence for the changing faunas of the world.

Ucko, P., and Rosenfeld, A. *Palaeolithic Cave Art*. Weidenfeld and Nicolson, 1967. A critique of earlier interpretations of cave art.

Wymer, J. *The Palaeolithic Period*. Croom Helm, 1985. An authoritative description of the worldwide evidence.

Index

Page numbers in italics refer to illustrations.